SONGS

The Mountain West Poetry Series
Stephanie G'Schwind & Donald Revell, series editors

We Are Starved, by Joshua Kryah
The City She Was, by Carmen Giménez Smith
Upper Level Disturbances, by Kevin Goodan
The Two Standards, by Heather Winterer
Blue Heron, by Elizabeth Robinson
Hungry Moon, by Henrietta Goodman
The Logan Notebooks, by Rebecca Lindenberg
Songs, by Derek Henderson

SONGS

DEREK HENDERSON

poems

The Center for Literary Publishing
Colorado State University

For information about permission to reproduce
selections from this book, write to
Permissions, The Center for Literary Publishing
9105 Campus Delivery, Colorado State University
Fort Collins, Colorado 80523-9105.

Printed in the United States of America.

Library of Congress Cataloging-in-Publication Data

Henderson, Derek (Derek Eaton)
[Poems. Selections]
Songs : poems / Derek Henderson.
pages ; cm. -- (Mountain West poetry series)
ISBN 978-1-885635-39-6 (softcover : acid-free paper) -- ISBN 978-1-885635-40-2 (electronic)
I. Title.
PS3608.E39255A6 2014
811'.6--dc23
2014035050
The paper used in this book meets the minimum requirements of
the American National Standard for Information Sciences-Permanence of Paper
for Printed Library Materials, ANSI Z39.48-1984.

1 2 3 4 5 18 17 16 15 14

Publication of this book was made possible by a grant from the National Endowment for the Arts.

ART WORKS.
arts.gov

This book is dedicated to my children: Charlotte, Peter, Audrey, and Alex.

I believe in song.
—Stan Brakhage

CONTENTS

SONGS

Portrait before the eyes, everything true in the lens. Her hands meet and equal. Serenity at the appearance of edges. Serenity was there before the eye roamed and is still here before the eye. Transparent storm door: the hand knows the window's evenness in a broken door (where the door broke it opens in a line, slow and bending), how the hot window cools, how the eye beholds and opens, how all's gone gummed up, gone human. Farther off, gathering in the heat, tinny like the doorbell's admission of American width, even there the eyes seem hidden in unwatchfulness as night begins to freeze, the window ledge begins turning to the ground, and the warm house makes a ceremony of its windows leaking heat. Ceremony is birth, heat dies in the window and cools off an inhabitant or two, the children run out of doors into an early-21st century, seeming to shine. In song, I become lyric heart, so, transparent. Singing meets up in the eyes in the knowledge that broken things abound in hope, the present is always beginning, an according, hoofclicks on the rooftop in June; how do we make the words? We wait. Song one is turnkey, tissue, a white yard, more American ground. Ground glass so far is heat, new working of heaven, identified and met in a snowy landscape, a high line bounding heaven. The eye grows an egg-like vault, swarm of fact in the heat, overply, heat fleeces the window with frost.

Portray the woman's reader, hands full of pearls, her silence is the product of her silence—she sails through a quiet house. Transparency colors everything: windows signed with breakage, the door is here for anyone, its clean lines, its billowing openness, its wooden lintel. Through the window a terrible image: stepping into the marriage chamber is Cain, dominating the solitude of night, this version of night —windows distribute starlight, the room fogs up its windows, the windows turn to paint an American scene outside, miles of newly planted rows turned towards the house. The first song is the window's song, too transparent. The song ends with someone tapping at the angles of the window's construction and the broken apple on the sill is fate's presence, branches outside are over everything, are ridiculous, a porous cover, just so. The first song is torque, matrix, water, roadways in May, completely American. A glass by the bed protrudes and announces water, the exact sound of a saint's passage through the room. The sky outside is huge, a complete frequency of color, there is color sitting by the window, a nightgown lain over a chair beside the window.

Pour out in the face of this mess of words. This hand is a word, cornered into writing all this shit out. To be anything before writing it is to be a thing in words I hold as ramification, ruination, home. Transparency flies laughing: under this window is breakage and shit—real shit, cat shit (buried far below, waste lining the yard, killing trees)—This window so streaked with blood hangs before my house and through it all I can see is America showing up all the same, warts and all, night blasted in the window, leading me to all the steps I find. A house with windows is portent of war, windows open onto America stretched to dearth, fully dried up.

This first song
stretched too thin already, a tiny candy sucked into transparency. This lens bends everything to smallness, halves our search into breakage, is held up too openly to unopening skies, the stars all hidden, floors turned up, kisses hesitant, built on words and words only,—what else can be so immanent? I lied the first time, I am made of tissue, a yard full of trash and weeds, fearful, always an American trying to get a leg up. Protrusion is my cup, my hateful filling up—I am a word that knows its own saying and is lost in all its shifting land, the sky could care less. I am huge with August, too full by half with scorn, overplied, seen in my window, writing this:

Retrace each letter of the woman's name. Lay miles of ink to zoom us to the occupations of bared fingers. The serenity of this woman rises into the serenity of place, a calm house. The eye glides, acetate its fluid cone, its aperture: the window was firm before its breakage—the window becomes terrible in the eye as image in the camera's opening, American symbol married in a visionary mouth, night foreseen, foretold, the window blank in its material, carried across, the camera is a useless window, the window keeps the hand spanning from its wrist in this American picture of distance and lack of presence. Nothing can occupy this zone like I do, the window my song, quiet, transparent. I lack a place to rest, lack something so quiet as the angel my eye already promised in the changeless tissue of breakage, the present falling off the boughs—I reach to it, burn for it, I cap myself off, whatever. This place is taken away, a missed kiss, a full yard, I am completely American. The glass protrudes and stops quickly, establishes stoppage to identify sand's passage—water-clock, too, a grand plan fully blown and frequent as St. Vitus' Dance. O, this layer is true, fine layer of flesh.

Try this again: impulse to speak gives pause to thought. As much as I occupy my space I am still, a tiny seed. The quietness of my thought comes up against the hum of space, the quiet house. Thrown from the transparent flow: yes, this is surely a breaking through (other things are pulverized, flow is not a straight line, not a constant wave, I swear)—and yes, this will be terrible to sum up in one sight, placed in the house locked and wedded to some pervasive American symbol of loneliness in expectation of night; and yes, this will be a branching out at last, the house will be so sought out, it will become a thing to sing about, an acme that cannot be put in print or English, or in the tight historic teeth of last year. Nothing will sing more than the words spinning about, sweet, *transparent*. I can say at the end: I heap up talk, the shit that spills out the mouths of angels, concrete as it figures itself out before its eventual brokenness; it is built and it is here and it is a done thing—the boughs let off cherry blossoms behind me, they cut into the new-built house across the way, this hum is only this or that possibility, and what is done in the boughs cuts the season off, discards tomorrow's snow-capped mountains; the first ceremonial turning of the key shows the new carpet already sullied, the boulevard behind more complete than the American dream that paved it past our house. We're calling a small war—I see you through the mean glass, gross and staring back at me, identifying yourself as me on the toilet, a saint passing back and forth to human. I'll be grand as I wash dishes while I look back at you watching TV, I'll see my self reflected in my window, in yours, in the window's reflection, in your TV, in my own admission of my own body.

Try the motherly speech again. Hands full of seed. The mother's silence follows alongside the silence of the whole story, of the last home left to us. Everything here is seen flying through everything else: windows and doors (the traffic of people, their collisions and straight lines, their stopping, their fleeing) — the window is a terrible imagination of creation married to the house, admitting a dead-ended Americanness, a penetration of loneliness instead of night — the window's black mirrors throw the room's light back at me, the house full of windows to use, windows firm against breakage, the hand reaches out and closes them to open them up — I am an American poet miles away, subject to distance. One open window is song, is lyric, sweetness, transparent. The song ends on top of a mountain of angel stuff, structured in the middle of breakage, made presence, bent, cut, almost razed,

like this: The first song is cut short layer and fulfilling yet

Wind as possibility.
The mirror is clear image
and color on the horizon
is blur: movements of apparent
light climb below
Earth in the window

Wind stabs below
lifts and shimmers the blood
lifts off the horizon's table
the camera sings
has swung down
the land holds over windows

The wind pulverizes me. I'm a rascal who shimmers in my own imagination and the heat of the season sullies me and makes me useless as the horizon always is—distant and hopeful only. Shift between the machines of my image and the machines that take my image. Earth opens up, furious, a window to itself.

Wind pulverizes. Risk scalds in the glossy shimmer before the eye and heat waste their sullen stretch to the horizon. The mouth scintillates, machine of photographic impulse. The earth is furious with the window. I can hear them rattling together.

Vents push out air from the dryer to the new wall. Heat shimmers between them heat in the middle of horizon. Mirage is nothing a camera can watch. Earth its own vent.

Wind in stuff. At its height it flickers in the heat in its height it opens up the horizon to a sort of wonder. The camera eats it up, the camera lingers and loiters and misses it all. The land heats up and builds its own wind.

Water flows. And now we sing perhaps too warily, keeping track of water's overflow. Breakage lovely and scattered: coke bottles and chalk. Crazed cityscapes (the streets are flooded, water hard to be held; water flows below its film, off the surface all is nicked and photographed as a word) blossoms lift off a branch, the same as the waters. Word breaks first in water. Songs come stiff, strong drink, sung with warmth; each crowns the previous.

Water is a flame. It burns as much as song yearning at its surface, acute and watery. Its colors favor breakage: bubble and cease, bubble and cease. The city before it is brief (life in flame, traffic relatively useless) film its sea-green windows which raise the state of the film, seamless purity of sameness with the water. Water is breakage in a word, I sing more regularly now, life is severer now, nothing but air in the vents and the relentlessness of song.

All water is river. The tallest mountains equal a crack in God, they are so much superficial sucking at the river. The core is my favorite place of breakage: all the chattery flow that comes out is heat. The city escapes, briefly (the roads are rivers too, and traffic pulls me into its flux); picture this — green water flowing over nothing but film, to continue in the sheer sameness of its own wateriness. Water is the hum of broken words. As we take two or three steps from the stark shore, life has no more heat than a cancelled first breath.

The water in the river. As full of movement as what two sets of eyes can see on the surface of broken water. Colors perforate each breakage: I can no longer call out in this heat. Brief city-scapes cross the surface (its streets like a river, the traffic its flow); passage of liquid-blue-green: in the same way we photograph nothing in its completeness in order to sculpt our senses in the sameness and continuity of water. Water is a verb of breakage. What calls us to pair, what calls us to three is rigid, severe: life is heat and its richness can't be seen by one person.

Hot water still splits me open. So there's nothing else left like the water that falls too hot to clean me as hot as the water was. My favorite clarity is breakage: the house opens me up to chalk on the sidewalk. Cut out the cityscape (the street cuts me off from houses across the street; the wall is not good neighbor; the storm drifting in, though, that I can handle); water will grow between us, a film that will wrap us up every night that water falls, the sluice continues to say what it has to say and the water we've got will get so hot as to burn us. Hot water works through houses and brings on breakage. Lay this out twice or thrice, it is still a grinning sign, strong and level with warmth I've already told you about.

Water is violent. Here it thickens in the channel and I see fish surface twice, searching water's height. They prefer breakage over color: their mouths taste air and call for change. Their brief passage into the breath of the city (the river is a road that flows, traffic troubles its surface only); their watery breath of the film below is nothing but everything—a camera can't make certain that moment they end the sameness of water. Water is always a word of breakage. The fish get a second chance and at the third are caught, go rigid, dead, they follow a road of riches to get them back to their start.

The stanza's strength is this: God's little gurgle (a dream of lowing cattle, all trussed up in rose— there's a rising laugh and amidst the rattling green there's nary a mean movement—it's a ballet, an invocation of innocence) is striated sequence, is structure of fire, illumination and furor, clearly placed. God out-plucks my plucking and everything announces autumn over Salt Lake City. It is still the outset of breakage—the world is automatic; it moves itself, I pass through with nostalgia. I am busy and idiotic. My contrarieties are all balled-up.

To this strong stance: an artery in the craned neck
(a sound of loosening care, sinews rolling around
in the collar, round head on top—everything
encounters a green world, and no movement is
slower in this ballet, this evocation of innocence)
a hoarse sound follows, each frame illuminates
what the neck pulls the eye to, the face pulled to,
locked, and everything painted in sober green,
in a childhood city, in breakage: world automatic,
cars pass by and nostalgia is idiotically busy,
now nothing contracts the kids dancing out here.

Two men stand and fart: the kids all giggle (a sunken dream, a lost carol, dressed in red, red thrown against everything, the growth of green (everything that is not green), and in the camera is an expansive ballet, an innocence) and come to abstract sequence where each mark illuminates a lock pulled and stuck; desire makes it so that pull outlasts the lock—at every point the lock dents but does not give in to the demands of *breakage* (what is this breakage?) in an automatic world, an automobile that won't start, nostalgia passes by, stupid and acting up against the women dancing.

I am twee, stark; I stand up: the kids spill over (in front of me a diver lowers himself, drowns himself, rides the waves, exists as ballast, till everything takes him in and grows over him, a long-time death, a slow bullet bringing waters to his shoulders) and everything abstracts itself, opens and folds, slacks and goes cold, sparking out in death, opens and pulls back, beckons. All over the house the rooms turn to garden, turn to the breaking open of shoulders: such winging out is automatic, the self moving into the world, a testament that history is idiotic. Stars begin to take over. All the turns are messages.

God is a strong line—the kids are betrayed (a dream that shuts us up, robes our tongues in red, bowls us over with its redness, everything pours against the green we voted for, it's in the moving sideways, a ballet, a claim to our innocence) and then there's a vague odor, each movement of the hand fills the room with a stench that lasts—a smell of shit that kicks us out of the room and pains us throughout the end of summer. In the first arrival of breakage: the world is automatic, it goes where it must, it lords itself over us and we forget how much of our occupation is stupid, given the slow dance of tulips that fills space between us.

Stars start to stand up: they spill out a kind of light (a trauma that lowers its song to us, that clarifies the turning of the earth, a turning that clarifies everything in turn, gaining us ground as it raises us up and in the long run begins us, a sort of ballet, choreography that overruns our stopped births) and we're taken out of what we're sure of, the light we let off tosses itself, strings itself out in distraction; the house throws us out into the wet grass and everything above us drives us down we're the children now, a broken building inside of us, automatic, the cars wield proof, the newness of this is memory until we figure out our idiotic swerves. I am gaining a spot to crash, I am beginning to touch the things that made me.

Parted. Here breakage begins to gain a human grace, so obvious at zero, a quantum of light, in greens and blues. O words get born to announce, exactly medicinal, photographic in the city of the naturalist. Mouths balance to the camera and its sweetness, o's hardly astonished enough to cry anymore. Moved to a happy exhaustion, a dear happiness for which I am not sorry. Piety precedes in or parts from an easy way, profound respect for pointing to the biology of movement—spiritual both ways, a disarming breakage of the literal tending to a religion of more; create here a book-sized seclusion (cut off opinion taken up and named "sensibility," named a divided thing) that entails a half-seen moment of God

Parted. Here breakage begins in the grain, as obvious as in the sea you see—light atomized in greens and blues. Birth is a word announced, exact as medicine, photograph of cities and mountains. Oscillations in the camera's film follow miracles of sleep—each frame follows a closed eye, a boy asleep at the world. Such strain is happy fatigue, faces are happy and they dream. Steps lead through a parting curtain and a screen door, the earth is full of repose, it contains spiritual and biological movements, and these steps through breakage are disarmingly literal and as religious as creation, pointed to from the margins of a small book (which spaces are believed to hold touch for sentiment and doubt) from which rise the heads of gods.

Bevel, bedevil. Here begins the moment that breakage begins to meet up with slicing and/or its broken vectors—there is such swift trajectory of glass, it gets hot as it breaks, as it flies out and corrals itself into dutiful slow fall, serrates itself in autumn light, in what's left of its greens and blues. The glass digs at the roots, takes advantage of the wood before it cools, in the midst of a sad awakening to its own ends. It'll die as a neutral sort of word, a heat-fired slice stuck in wood, like a flash-bulb popped and broken open. Summer wilds it up through the tree's roots, grows its gloss up through its trunk and sends it skyward. Glass gets to be a kite this way, gets lucky in the end to be locked in its height, gets to die aloft and hidden. This is the faith of breakage: that, failing all else, it allows me elusiveness; Eleusinian depth ever biding in the stillness of biological insertion (how does *I* get in there?): don't blink—I'll have an arm raised against me and a hammer's little tink to find me godly, sitting forever in the all-consuming wood of an unsawed tree—I'm a cretin (here I am out and aloof—a door not caring for its opening, but with one more twitch I'll fell this fucking tree . . .) tied up in the worst way, in a sudden God, no signs to show . . .

Crouching here in the breakage I begin to learn the use of grains scattered in evident dance, a swirl of piecemeal light slanting up and below. The beginning is a word denouncing the medically exact, photographs with nothing of the sun inside. The oscillation of waves saves the appearance of this moment as photograph, shrugging off the stunned stance in this, the world's first moment. The glass small and extreme with the tired houses, I see hours as souring. The wisdom of breakage lifts me up and crouches me down, so it is elusive, deep, seen and seen again, a sound spiritual and biological, in the moment all God's disarming manner collects and I see it form in space as a heated sickle (it is not a cross of gold to be touched with feeling and doubt) crossing over the gorge of God.

Burp and fart. Here the teeth break apart, get broken on each kernel, this is so very planned, an atomization in each klunk of each tooth against each blown breath, so it's felt as often as breath. The wind leaves the body and is a sloughing off of speech, we're in the middle of this now, I'll take a photograph (picture) to send it back to you so that the world might know your shiftings. The wild swinging of the camera selects an understanding of the black that is kind enough to keep the world out. As for me, I'll raise a kite in the winds' brokenness before I spit out some elusive and shitty fate. I respectfully swallow whatever spirit is given me, and my biology will take it all in and swallow it and make it stop in moments. I'll abide by the shit I feel sent flying and so I'll form a way to put it all into jars and save it and display it (the glass is no church, no place for me to be sentimental, no way for me to bury words inside of other words), I'll die with whatever last word God sends me. It's the word he sent.

Get out. I mean go. What I've broken is beginning its own use, a seed clear to its own quantity—it is clearly zero, it is clearly the smallest particle of light, neither true nor speeding away. The word—a particle itself—was born the second it was announced; the word—like particle—was a core for stillness. Caught in film, it was a cure for film. The camera catches the movement—it is the dumbest child we've birthed. In the end, I love it, happily—I love its sordid stopping. At last, I pity it as paradise, respect the depth with which it catches spirit and body in a moment and sends their broken forms seamlessly into a literal religion like a dug-up body breaking through the earth (I believe I'm saved and static as it moves without feeling or doubt)—I'll turn aside to the goldenness of God.

Duel of fools. What appears in the forest is a flower that rustles, is a large gradation in the layer of leaves, aligned to deer prints, across coincidences of insects. It has *your* manner, is as important as your history, it intersects with what it can.

The sky falls. What else? Even blown
rose blooms catch the eyes. Air digs,
and fulgurant white streaks thread
and sear the hot Astroturf welcome
mat, then roll back, cornsilk wherever
insects shine, a manner of madness,
such languid thin coals shot through
with sunset overextending the valley.

I'm a fool. In this I resemble the forfeit of flowers rounding around and attending to the gentleness of my dissection of this tree (I'm a shard of glass, recall—a bit of poison searing and roiling in the tree from root to stem—across which I fill it full of manner. Still, important though I am, I'll grow sore and spend myself coursing down its phloem, up its xylem. Yuck, yuck, yuck.

Tramping across the earth. There was a way that words bloomed with peach blossoms that made it a plain net to house the words that read it. You see the White Stag in its leap, then over it a ripple of air building to white, so whitening we are in a dawn creeping, a tone heard over the quiet.

Spoil the world. If each thing assimilates to every other thing, it is therefore a forest on fire and what runs through it is vulgar and detested, and each little hole in it is a hole in its surface and rolls back against the better sense of whatever anyone in there can feel, a beginning creeping against whatever *you* can feel.

I'm spilling, a fool. The mouth is an opening like a flower in bloom rushing into life and beginning to sear, a challenge to the linoleum, oh, that's a static thing and I'm up against the error of faith, or rather of manner,—how can I count on the importance of things that creep across the same things you see.

Blank sand and still ocean. Gliding facts over facts. Four breaks in the façade equal this: surrounding leak. Heat oversees its own beginning—give over to meet the four slicings of wood as givings-over, broken-rhythmed and intersheaved as you get clear of the upper layers of water, of sand. Slicks on the surface speak of windows, an end of your strength, westerly winds, flittering silvery light.

Without a frank kiss to let you go, you eye the Pacific. Your eyes glide around in your face. For the breakage of a face is just this: something else to stitch up. The sea is plied over with the first of day's moments, an intersheaving of broken rhythms on the colored surfaces. Only the windows speak, brusque love of the eastern sun, instant silver light.

Nothing left to say and I'm okay with that. Cut this off, the facetious bent of the shit I'm saying. From here on out, breakage is façade. I tell you, thus: where you stand is a place to sit. Quit your goddamn walking—the merest wind, you know, could knock you down and make you sing. My broken-rhythmed switching in the veins of this tree leaves me in bits brought to the farthest leaves, and now I'm over everything—God, so I feel. A nearby window says something, I am hid and braided with the west-setting sun, grilled in sylvan light.

Saffron a flower of ease. It comes, faces the scored surface of plowed earth. Beside the breakage a building rises in gusts of faith: its corners are the seams of its trace. The sea is a gate for feet, it parts the right way before the construction site, a surface on a surface of broken-rhythmed rhythms in superficial colors. The sun is everywhere and the window proves this, uses its glass tone as reflection of everything as accident, loose, silver, instantaneous.

Without our easy sight, or our easy peace. Cut it up, make it into delicate fragments. For each breakage is a façade and in just this way: the juggler is always exposed. O sea, bring me down alongside you so I can taste how you are built, a salt dispersed across your surface and sent into broken rhythms of colors above all. Sometimes I can't leave anything behind but the film of my skin, and it always layers itself on my back—what I see rising across the land is nothing but flash.

Nothing is easy or clear. I'll tuck it all away and reveal only facets. Every facet broken, just so: it's a system of tape breaking down. The sea splits itself up against the front of a sand castle, it takes sand down layer by layer, a broken-rhythmed coloration: tan to brown, brown to beige, colors all fucked. We're only left with the wind, dying down as the sun sets: loss is stars spreading out.

Animated ocean. Poisons, tortures, stretchings, angles. The sea of song is entry of spring. Late in the year, beautifully dumb beautifully profound. The break attains a turn away from the elemental, where song comes unhinged, placed in metaphor. The loveliest chance we have is here.

Seated here. Fish and children hum over all. The sea of the last song reaches from a stuck place, then ties you up in testament of words. Breakage is not error in the elemental dens; in the dens songs flash in the outerference of an insistent word. Eyes zoom constantly in all these songs.

No longer even mere animal. Not fish, tarantula, errant goose, angle of incidence. The sick sea is house, a held zone, and I am static, inserted, at best a gust of wind holding below. Breakage rages above me, elemental, I dive and no longer see sequence as organized, everything I am is metaphor. One thing is small and beautiful, it can't be lived in, I search

Movement mars. Little crosses, spiders in the lawn's sun, engines. One can say farewell to the marring, the heavenly force of its entrance, or feel it arrive, a profound and direct pain. Breakage aligns itself on the side of the elements, one day it will follow song as a glowing out. I'll do nothing but sing, then.

Animals in the sea. Fish, turtles, long worms, angled crabs. The sea is a song to heaven, and here we've gotten into it, immersed ourselves in the right way, deeply as all its inhabitants. Breakage always happens below its element, and then we try to sing ourselves out of the effects of metaphor. One of the most lovely songs is this one.

All I see is dire. Vision, cold pattern, a sought rift, pale beginning. Heat overseas heaven laying down in the caught-up throat, just there, right near the day tipping down. Breakage breaks by air, water, sun, earth; where it folds in I fall down, a metaphor for my words, open and failing. Even the water, my sign, says so.

A comical masterpiece. Comely mouth, fully bound to festival. Three themes work so strongly we can't neglect them: a writing of *Rhinoceros* in the broken window (just so veiled as glass becomes guillotine) projects such an awful fall, it's so close to the beginning that we take each gushing as a hope, a lately belied lie. Second, the children, lying under blankets, splayed, splendid. In the shadows is a held spirit—silhouettes of birds, butterflies, alligators, boxers—all these turn in shadows on the walls all night, the sky outside names them, keeps them in a middle category, fingers wagging have cast on the wall the things they love: an end of art, a held spirit, a Californian drawing in the middle of the night, on white walls; so we are so enthusiastic, so ingrained in artifice that all the world is married to our benighted nuptials. So with such blue shadows we build (whoever knew all the breakage and all the fills—all these damn years of attention, the shut blinds opened, denuding all the wall, all we knew) shadow puppets, in our ears engender a special movement, that is so foolish, —that the geese we spread honk their horns and there is straightaway a magic. The rhino shreds the hands, the children splay their hands in the warm house whenever the whitest part of the wall unspools like film. The breakage constrained as width widens and narrows, glass against which words are written in white, words which spread in shadows. Third, the rhino is all rolling Energy; the children laze, bound by their action, they are the art man sees in Energy, that rests on empty coasts, a youth that mills about, toothless as it must be. Nature, Civilization, unspool, change with their laughter. Worklessness, Fantasy, Frivolity. Or else: in their hands is *Romance* and *Rhino* and *Window* and the unfoolable children are what Romance forgets, that is, what remains the same in you, what is stolen in you. The rich language of breakage is a tactic stemming from advantage, the turn to swerve. In an Other grows a spreading web, belief in the same sort of reach which is criminal in man.

One more bit of earth to cross, cosmic bit of dirt. Commas, festival of union. Trees time out an unstable, unmistakable, immediate sound: a scent of new sap shines through, current through the window, open and broken (a giant open mouth). Yes, the sun spins too, as you call out to me, clear and springlike, a measure of the sea level from the last song. All the children's mouths stained with Kool-Aid and perfectly naked, laughing. All mouths send sound forth, open every day: codices of categories, and each participant a center, an avenue of rings, scanning the volumes of life. One species is different from another, draining argument of force; they both move in fine, enthusiastic blue (my dear breakage over it all, the most secular diocese, its silhouette is possible use) and string themselves up in the dark: at a certain and special moment, a car's honk causes everything to disperse. A nose in the center of the face, my child is an easy distraction going into the house, the sound of water spilled in a broken glass on the floor. Genitive. Each innuendo of each footstep of each failure of the modern motion picture. I turn the TV off. Breakage is an elaborate construct, let every point of my body sense it. I charge a brutal energy, pure; my son, source of union, the sound of a general energy that returns me to a new state, my head rested on the wall, considering nothing but his flight. Nature, civilization, an experiment with the jokes I carry around. Reality is imagination and frivolous. O: let the sound out, stories and the force of them out through the window and let the child be clear in the sound that each story should be right there up against him— I sense the brokenness unmoving and how different it is from strategy. In this spring wind I love in large part womanly, and remain doggedly masculine: there is nothing left but laughter.

Um, masterpiece is comic? Cosmos, a festival of unity? I'm very scared so I try to order everything immediately—this is all mediated. I am a rhinoceros passing delicately through breakage (the marketplace is instantly guilloutined), I project myself through my hide, I am as prominent as a deep-sea creature destined for eating. It's all creeping up on me, nonchalantly and impudently; I despise it, I jog around avoiding it. I'm evidently encased, blossoming is not for me, I'm classed among the mute things, and participate among them, trying to hold onto my arrangement of my bound-up life: I'm a different sort of casement, a drawn-off body of hot sex, if anything; I'm all encased, an enthusiast, but of a different sort, a requiem of each dead light in each dead nuptial. Such silhouettes as we (what more breakage can end this, send it into a fraction of hiddenness, put me to use in this silhouette?) find ourselves in is special momentum, as perilous as a goose's honk that dispels the magic it rises from. O nosing around, you pass me off as faithful, as an easy jog around the park, and the innuendo of feeding ducks is as witty as the feeding of ducks. Breakage builds to an elaborate grace, but to be lit up with any manner of voice is to snuff around a new marriage of any two things newly met?—it's too precious and I'll never be able to begin that again. Civilization, naturally, is going along too tentatively. And so am I. Whatever, motherfucker. Realistically, imagination is frivolity. OR: Where you build romance, there the rhino in us forces its way through the cracks, unfoolable as a Romance in the cold logic we've arrived at. O, dear sense of breakage, of humor more difficult than my tactics: I'm breaking away from the idea that your humor might peel me away from my more feminine parts, might make me remain doggedly masculine, all alone in my own laughter.

An open door over the linoleum. The mouth opens, a festival of union. So much more is given you, an immediate collection: a round night thing, establishment of steps across broken glass in the door (now there is much to cut), protection of your feet, something as simple as fish in the glass bowl resting on the cabinet. Then children, outside and not listening to the openness, too much at play inside it. Then a body, outside the doors and in the night, the very apex of participation, holding what remains to be retrieved, arrow to the eyes: a divers body, drawn from the heat of sex and want; all forms invest in a certain specie that requires air and moon for the change we count on in breath. The body is blue silhouette (wanting only breakage and apex since the clock announced us, but what can silhouettes use?) hanging at a certain moment, *especial,* as dangerous to itself as the mouth opening to speak quiet spells. The profile establishes steps out the door, the child's happy play now inside the house, an insinuation of all that has dispersed in the current. Picture the moment of breakage: the structure of glass in pieces before the broom, how it is all laid out later in a manner of use. The moon an assembly of rays, an energy passive, pure; children's location in union, they too are a species of energy that knows the articulation of bones below skin, that hold only as they begin. Civilization is a natural gesture of their play, of toys they hold. Imagination in the moonlight is easy and real. The moon, the mouth, the open door and its empty window: the abiding reach of the Romantics and the wind roiling through open spaces, through frames, and the children unspool their abilities down the driveway; as soon as they're gone, I choke up. I can laugh at the broken glass, but this is a dangerous strategy. In a sense, my blood is in large part material, moonlit, and the rising of laughter in me merely masculine.

One grapples with mastery. Each pause in the construct its own festival. Draw your themes into words so they might pale in the middle light: heat passes evenly and re-sets itself in the midst of heated breaking (now, at least, we see the guillotine): motion opens up the word that is become the thing as word, the soul is yes a heated word and we die as we speak it, but only insofar as we lie about it, as we swallow what is primeval. Give off the kind of opening, nonchalantly and impudently naked, that spills you into heat. Then go into whatever works, and take your time with the night as it passes; it might let you call yourself out in the middle of everything as it happens, even death; it's all true, it shines in a way that isn't yet lit up for you. I'll trust your enthusiasm to outlast you when you die in the heat of a hot kicking against death where man makes his marriage outside his home—this might be true. In this way I'll become a blue silhouette (I'll die in the midst of this breakage and become the culmination of sense as an attention to the trees in the yard—is this ever something I could break?), I'll be hung in the middle of some special and open blank that is so far away it will call to me as if with a magic horn, and everything will be played at once.

Here comes the timing of the air I inhale, here come the kids spilling so luckily into room's magic, a room so full of light that everything plays off of every surface. The heat reaches a charging tempo, the children spill luckily out of the house, my ankle is the tiniest instance of the force of my leg and waist and in the end it swings out too modestly for this film. Breakage lifts itself until everything is even with its extensive grip—I'm too full of heat to even know how I'm constructed anymore and I leave everything to you all, dear reader. I'll stare the heat down my nose, a sort of brute energy; the kids use what comes to them and use it well, I'll sign off in the heat as a sort of energy—I'll cure it and damn the cost I've installed an air conditioner in the middle of the window, in the middle of the night, I'm beginning to meet what I'm supposed to figure out. This is difficult, this bullshit saving, this lopping-off of the hands I was given. I'll work hard from now on I swear I'll bleed myself of my frivolity. Oh, God: the heat weighs on me, it's driving me, I roam into my array of zeros and I'll look out the window and I'm a child and fool and unfoolable and I see the roaming of what speeds in the best of ways, it is coming to meet me. The best kiss I've known is now breakage between two breaths and I'm still a modest motherfucker in my strategy. I've even left behind the details of throwaway hours and fuck it all here I'm still trying to latch the door after all this

A shade over the earth, a comet over the house. Comet, festival of speeding matter. Try this theme on, establish it immediately or at last: zero in unrepentantly on the window's breakage (it holds up, beautiful guillotine) to project a little ways past it, on what is also before it, the cracks were made in the third song. Little kids ponder the break and rejoice with new insolence. A little marriage before the doors in the night, the push, the swish of all the participants against this audacious sky—they throw their arms up wide: it is another sort of marriage, drawn up from a calling out to *be;* they will sort this out fervently, they will certainly sort, who will drink wine under moonlight for their vows? There is a blue silhouette (but who makes breakage their uttermost end, despite the never-ending 20th century; who makes use of breakage against the silhouette?) and puppets dance around in a certain special moment so dangerous that an alarm disperses all the magic. The parent repents, the children laugh uproariously in that part of the house where they insinuate ghosts from a recent movie. The breakage is strewn across the floor, a pleasant array, for it is not important in what way you view it anymore—it is broken. The outer edge of the zero, its line is pure, brutal energy; the children come and go with the house, in the house, they are a sort of energy that sends new love out to each object—each chair, each spoon, each bowl of sugary milk—they ensure that each moment will never have to begin again. Nature, civilization—they are active experiments in *play*. Reality, imagination, a frivolous distinction. Where—*here*—they are wedded to the story of impulse, the window never fooled the children as a story to frame and separate the inner from the outer. To laugh with them at its breakage is a different strategy. It is their moment of humor, there is no place here for mother or father in their laughter.

In a roomscape, perspective—the point of sight—is a photographer's seduction. The machine photographs proofs posted over there, below the window to the right of the bathtub, a measure of the house where life happens outside. Casually, we become anchored at the extremest point beyond the window, we walk in the steps of the photographer.

A room scraped to the point of opinion as the photograph senses itself. A camera encounters places to hear, sells ears on each stage of the comfortable adjustment of a house outside its life as recorder. O randomness, begin to escort me to no extraordinary place, let wind place the photograph's decision.

A room scraped clean, unless the point you're looking at it from is a photograph that is still left on the floor. The camera took a picture of an encounter with *place* and this is what you see, and you buy into the easy steps that adjust you to a house that has all its life gone out of it. When you leave this house, you'll follow a road through boughs of trees and into a hidden room at the far end of town. There's no goddamn ocean waiting there, awaiting thee, and your feet will still at times incline themselves to the picture

In a space of escape, I stand and walk out from the portrait I'm sitting for. The camera blinks my route onto its plates, signs my standing comfortably; even as I leave the house light kisses level film. The walk I take wanders, deathly, and I leave behind a door on rusted hinges: in the photograph, the words come true, wandering, cord-like.

A room to escape, a point of view from a lens, everything is here to be said. The photo appears to bring an end to everything we see, and sends us into comfortable bits of tape that one can adjust in a house of dead-ends. What I see from the corner only gets me out so far as the ends of my eyes; at least I get so far as my footsteps can't be photographed.

A room in its escape, with a point selected for the placement of a camera. The camera finds its place and shows you and sits you down to lead you over to stand at your own height; in this way you'll find your way out. Your pratfalls bring you to an end before you can stand back up again—in here you'll find how still you can stand, how you can wait for the photo that comes.

The depth of the skies
(seen from breakage is "unique delay
to voice") is like traffic at night.
Before the dawn interrupted,
it seemed possible to suppose
(but what was born was crime)
mouth against mouth makes brilliant
structure of saintliness, of gods crossing;
a film that cures lightly,
remains and material of two fireflies.

The suck of a kiss (to which breakage is a unique sound, as of a mirror) seen here as traffic in the night. The fall went on into spring, but I could not imagine time as possibility (mothers losing children); I tell myself in the glancing light that only light can change; the picture makes itself die down in the light, and sends out a question of how light comes about.

Fuck off into the sky if that's what you want (it never was, and you've broken off from my own breakage: "I've reneged, yes, on going out with you"—that's a keen way to say divorce) tonight. The kid of our erstwhile fucking is *not* a word we made up together (you mothered him and couldn't talk and so should know); he is a held thing, and now he can paint his own words, select them more or less true; we filmed his birth with light from the window, you bled out your pain, I saw a field of fireflies,

Fuck off, she says (because breakage is "the only thing left I can see") and I see this as an approach of headlights in the night. The first source of our problems pour out to become divine (milk a spilled nourishment); the glints of light culminate only in deflection; the film on the floor —here I question the remainder of littler lights, of spilled milk.

It's all sucked off into the skies (so far away it's warm, it's another sort of breakage, "this engine gone, now you're better off without it") so these places get farther off as the night goes on. The stopping places I choose cannot reveal the name for the place I sit (I mutter, I'm kind of far-gone); still, I've got a rock that is a word hefted to its height and I can throw it through your window; your window is lit up with burning words and I believe that each angle of the rock takes me a little bit higher, makes me a little bit luckier.

Low suck of the skies (the breakage you see it through "is the only sound that keeps you here") has come like traffic in the night. The first fount is not possibly possible, it is not something to dive into (not a mother feeding her child); I point out the slight gathering light spread across the field like echo; the film of golden light lets me know light brushes up against itself to remain an aspect of itself.

The first song discolors. A study of an airport in fog, all the lines blurred, fantastic travelers, searching reflections in the windows. A first film for spies. The airplane is not a machine that can break by degrees and its place is alien, inhospitable, arcing nowhere.

Stay here in the clear loss of sound. Eyes study where light rests in mist, all the empty house is lined with sparks and corners, here I slip and begin. Begin to go in spin. Here the veil is tugged in passing, a mechanical and broken gesture, and I see that heaven is at war with itself: a grasping reach, a gesture that pulls nothing up.

The first song is always without color. It is a song of airports, of boulevards, everything lined along a burned out house with phantom voyagers, reflections of age and grasping. Begin a spy film: The airplane is not a machine we ever trust to break, and still is warlike, aggressive, a place we can't live in, cold and motile locus. Good luck.

Here is where I loosely put down my watch. I am a student of a flown heaven and no bells; all that's behind the house now is laundry on the line, set in sail by the wind, spinning along in time to my reflection in the window. I am a toothless spy in this film. The beeping beep is not a ghost to watch over me, but a machine of breakage, and I see a tear open up in the blown bedsheets—what is alien is not otherworldly; what is art is kitsch.

The first song was always in color. I can see an airport amidst clouds, everything is lined up to get out of the house, a vigorous pause in fantasy, a reflection of the world in its segments. At first, I spied the world in film. The airplane then left contrails and I knew it as a machine that loved its breakage; its flight is always relative to its distance, its hostility, its arc.

For once, sound is in color. A mess to do and an arrow pointing the way out—everything in line with the house with the bent roof, with the fallen ghost, with architecture reflecting its own stance. We'll eat in here on filthy dishes and never notice what spills in. O flight, bear me up and away—be my machine untouched by breakage and send me to alien parts—it's inhospitable here, arc me away

Wandering train after wandering train meet slowly and thunderously in the heat of a Midwestern landscape—warming ember and clanging tussle of crossing rails, God's heaven-bound words get photographed. An eye tears up in study of American motive, met by a clearing in works both broken and pixilated (brown, red, blue, gray). Eyes met at last in the still pose, in the driven walk.

The train moves in a photograph of a moving train, where little more than the passage of time in the Midwest is perceptible in the waving grain that passes by. A stillness uncovers an American movement, with broken colors, everything pixilated in brown, red, blue, gray. Arms reach up to a calm sky where clouds float.

Beside the wet mold, I tug on the camera's trigger—this is before the buttons and I am beside the mold and such, with a shutter that is slow enough to catch the mold in the middle of its growth and I know I can bring it back home in some form though not as warm as here as it shifts through the air and fractures our weakening resolve. It's an awful heft, the cherished, studied end in an America just beginning, with the fairest of the fair breaks as broken as Picasso (brown, rotten, blown: "grown," you say). It ends with a run at the sky (not really—it's fucking earthbound, it's grown over with weeds).

The hand's tremolo caught in the photograph by trembling hands, moving together at a low point in the land, a distinguished Midwestern field, fried copper, tan fragile. One studies the seeds unstrapped from their casings, their movement American drift in heat; one picks at the grains, breaks them open at first, then rustles them, blows them into the dirt, leaves them, grows them. Stars hide behind the calm of a blue sky, a giant gallery of small, still clouds.

O from motions of you, photograph, oh your movements are form, like a mouth opened to the passage of drawling speech, knowable only by the most hidden drifter. I study how the house was raised, it is an American movement, at its core broken and picaresque—you got your house higher than mine (and bazoom, good for you, it's true—you're higher to God, in the blue, succinct). You reach as far as you can with a quiet, subtle fluttering of your hand. It's as good as silence

He is trained to move as a photograph
is trained to move, by feet, through
whatever passage he sees himself within.
His going is foregone consequence.
He studies eyes raised up
an American moment colors
quickly broken picked apart
(bloodlike rolling reflecting gray sky)

we wait in the sky held floating by cloud-cover

Abstraction completes a perfect normalcy: culture's devices, the microscopic grains of things, fluttering light passes through cells —like all the sections of paint breaking off the walls, an arrangement of color as savage as what we are given to see. Rain sloughs in gales, anger of paint at its exposure, seizure in a second. Only a man with limitless energy and risky innovation can approach such effort.

Abstraction, after all, a natural bit of this: a forming culture, seen in full, in miniature, a kernel we can know in shadows cast by the moth in the basement—we're all broken into pieces as the moth flies into the light, a fantasy of wild passage, what man can be unlit in this? The play of shadow is a gallery of our stretched-out sitting, search for our seeking. There is no one end when energy ends, and nothing is lost when we find the words to hang any risk above us.

Sky's the limit, right? I'm permanently neutral: closure is a way to shut me up, I'll grant the microscope its thing, its shadowy eyelash in front of its lens will let everything ultimately pass beyond the veil of film, right?—it's as relative as everything I've ever said about breakage, a fantasy of color, redemptive as a little imagination. Fuck that shit and split it from me—I am a gallery full of pictures hung haplessly and seditiously at every turn. I'm a sultan and I'm alive in infinite energy returning to some sort of source.

Carry away a natural perfection: cultures do mold us, our great and small parts, cut us in pieces like moth's wings strobe porch lights—it is still movement we pick out in the shadows—like all the pointed, broken frames, we are a fantasy at the moment of our salvage, like all that *can* be seen. Diving into the breeze, moth encounters gale, pint-sized body gusts away from its disease for a second. Sometimes a man gives all his energy to invent all that he might carry.

Get out of the way, because it is perfectly natural: cultures mold themselves, the microscope of God is huge and you are just a grain in the middle, a fluttering thing moving against given light — like all the last layers of paint breaking open in bubbles, a fantasy of color as redemptive as any you have imagined. Only the outside has any energy at last, invention has nothing to do with the arrangement of force.

I'm set aside, a broken man among men, naturally: culture is a worm, curled beneath a dingy microscope: even when it alights as a moth, it is empty of its cells.—So we're all still children, each left to lift what's left of breakage, even the fantastically clear and wild bits that insist we can stand above them. We end up shying away, to find clearing in the stilled engine sending blood through the body. You are selected by blood that races through you—energetic, uninvited to the race, dirgelike, spanning the risk of your life.

A cycle of songs, the last needs of a cut stem. Portraits of robbers, killers; of Gold; of burn and rot; of a cool curve in black and white, one of a lurching gang in array after array of ghosts, thrown from there to here, working the light, thrown out and slung south and raised up like lightning hits the clouds, a giant shifting. In each engine is shift, low gears clear away into limit, into messy intake and exhaust; over there is creeping and aching in the dark and in the light and halfway to negation is . . . what? A halving of *way* — a halving of a handsbreadth, everything afraid that speech might be locked down: today is a sculpting of angels on a dark field. Portraits of words with girls and boys all broken so the bird sings — a canary, perhaps — and then a hound nosing into the ground. The day arrays, is effulgent on the clear windows sending red and yellow against the wall; the air is bare, there is nothing but dust kerneling the air — the air is filmy, flimsy, here is all golden corny light, there's nothing here to unfurl — green and blue tints in the ether a dose of breaking out, duration gone Godwise, a magic cheat, a self-built barricade against self's samenesses. The blowsy dress, kneeling in August already, with July behind and January behind, this year June sent a new winding, a new wind, and I've barely photographed it: this is my material, the genius of this place is a sort of caving in. A few songs left.

Ceiling for our singing, a first ramification and a principle gamble. Take back the stars in a corner of the sky, they're all gold in this haze, the color going brown and red, the color of theft; my calling is clear in nothing and in white, a sense of continuation stretches to stretch, like a dream of a mouth at its widest point, a mouth speeding to furious flash in the face, anything like a sound makes it clear as a roar to begin a lecture; theft begins to peel, anchors in nothing, a blank frequency, a regulated evocation of sincerity—test of the poet,—the solid ground is a sculpted angel. I retract the sound fighting to leave my mouth and the children are all still broken, birds in a little cage. The sequence deepens page by page and crystallizes in eloquent sound; the seed's use is a picked fruit I eat like seed—light fighting victoriously in the first instance of fire. Ether and fire in the house, leftovers of breakage, crossing everything with God, the knowledge of God as magic, i.e., everything visible now, bodies invisible. Pure passion is echo, white is what is photographed, June is ragged and June lasts and is new and bullish, and the heat haze separates possibility from the genius of the place, a sort of crazy beginning. One loves the song still.

It's a cycle of songs at first loving and at first quick. Return us to the oblique source, dear sound, dear murmur, dear stolen bit of flower; make it all more clear in petal and branch, nothing more than continuation, as if from frame to frame, as a ghost might make itself material amidst broken glass on the living room floor, as it might here, pushing angrily against the flash of the raging cameras that try to capture it, against anything that might make it seem to have a clearer place. What am I supposed to do now to alleviate the struck frame? I could have not slammed the door, or broken the window, perhaps; better yet I could have started and not broken, and perhaps have freaked a little less or not negatively so—evoked a sincere tension that I might now call poetic; or I could have wielded myself as angel, or at least the sculptor of one. My mouth interspersed with coursing wine and brokenness, a bushed bird flew through with each opening of my mouth. Sequence follows, a weeping of eloquent bullshit tears—I ought to have used a picture to grade how well my tears caught in the moonlight, dancing on my face. Am I this impertinent still, is it true that I've fallen this far and let this folly fill my latest book, as if out of the ether; is this the newest, latest, last breakage, after all? Does God still know the magic that fixes me? Sheer peacefulness is a hole in a five-yen piece photographed flying down a well in Kumamoto Castle, in March—we were childless then, or we were on our knees together and endeared, or else we never were and were ever so, or we were bodies separated by touch and genius and we were sort of dearly split apart. I was always a love song—

Circle of cars arrayed at first in a vast line before they're rammed down on the table. Try this again: here is a key, goldish, the color of the deadbolt in the door, robbing the lock of its house; clean the Formica to show its squares in black and white, without accounting for how they're all marked and remarked, and now a phantom of alcohol materializes here, here it is, and it accelerates in a flash to redden the guests' faces, each one face clearly lined and suddenly speech is assumptive: I call away from the certainty of my error, tense little poetics—the solid angles of the steps lead up and around a corner. The bathroom is low-ceilinged and also tiled in black and white, though in a negative frequency below—Try this (*what?*) again: the drop ceiling drops from water's weight, I bathe in my sleep and the tub runneth over, a mixture of my brokenness and my paternity and my marriage and my house; ladybugs fly to the walls. Padre the cat hides in cupboards and flees through the window. The sequence of my calling out is crystal clear, clear as electricity; grainy texture is incidental to the film of water on the floor, the lights overhead spark and pop, dance around the first plant my son ever grew. I resort to holes, to golden sight in the broken ceiling, across which little water gods seep their magic, making me invisible. Passion scrapes the eye with photography's equivalence, change is as much an ache—change and duration are: new wine in the mouth is material to connect talent to genius, saint to courier.

This is a love song.

Even the cycles have lied, and even your erstwhile take on them has left you groping and stammering. It's a sad treatment, you've also been robbed and in a certain sense killed, good, you've been brought out onto that road we mentioned earlier; I'll level with you — it's clear that all my words so far have been known somehow already, — they materialize themselves in a scrawl that flits itself into something known and felt already; what you wanted to know was already clear, you saw it as a law, a love floating before you and speaking to you; you heard the little kid screaming in your arms, you took on the swearing in of wit (I mean the slipping of these words into the negative, their evocation of everything that spans their definition — you know exactly what I'm talking about)

It's the heat that sculpts us into angelic leftovers. We carry our words with us in the hopes they might mean more than what we say, we know at last we're broken little kids, birds flitting away, days chasing after them. The opening and unfolding of any crystal-clear word is a well-spoken one. I've broken every rule and collected here the goings-away of my language as film crossing its source of light, its source of being. Everything goes more full, a bladder set to piss, air set to break over our heads, there is a door to God, and it's just the work of a little man like me, there's only so much I can make do. I'll serve my heart's stock and go wherever my movement tells me to go, I'll go and I'll endure, I'll know new heights, I'll lift myself to the gesture that gets me photographed, I'll be degraded, I am the warmth of my material, the heat I give my body, I am that talent for being in my place, I am __________ a saint of movement that never sits still. I am a lift, I am a lie. __________

One sees the songs clearly, each a first branch of a first tree. They portray the tree carrying us to golden entrance, burning red robbery; my calling out is clear, blank and white, it lacks the continuity of the tree's branching arms, its armaments, phantom of spring that keeps its icicles, keeps them here and sends the sun in flashing rage through the icy clarity of the air: there is a certain sight of sun that accelerates—it flashes and rages on the eyes—it supposes that it will properly thaw; the theft is clear, it is black and white, and is often framed in the negative, an evocation of the tenuous place of the poem; the melting is thus angelic, a sculpture of loss in loss. These portraits are overall losses of marriage, offspring of breakage, slow yellow light chained in its disappearance. The ordering of drip is crystalline eloquence: it employs grain after grain of light, leaves a film of water in which the grains grow and wilt in an instant of gold, there is a dance on a fallow field that turns, resorts to fertility, a plain of water that waits on its breakage, for God to instill his unquiet magic; the puddle rendered evident. The thin passion of the sky with its lack is photographed in June with the boys, and June lasts and lasts, the new middle time of our hours, it is a substantial month and sets up the swift genius loci, the sort of caring that is always vagrant. A love song.

A little bit left of a series. The beautiful character of breakage as the machine stops taking pictures; I am a movement so guided, conducted from side to side, to the fore and the aft, a pulsation of movement, a beating heart and all the vectors and spines shush a little bit with each gesture—alarm is a test of order. Breaking to touch the little fatuous dear, I strengthen my sense against the sounds of my organs as they stop and include leaving out, the ease of a hand (it's so natural this ceasing, always flying into its own capture by design, faith is an intrusion inside me and I am still a child of the sea). Green in the body, still a song, like a partly loved joke, orgasm as a precisely-aimed interval. In others is movement to song tuned to the sea, all these directions turn to pull a new seed from the salt depths, implicating gravity, the fall of seed; I concede morality to breakage—a sounding inside me. Nothing left but seed time and a sense of recollection—we never dropped seeds, goddamnit. Colors, figures, rhythms: train each passage to nothing but stars —the breaking came no more real than the purest form of *fall*.

O but series is beautiful. O but writing is beautiful, characteristic of breakage in a ceaseless camera; movement reaches apex and always comes back down, the side I chose is a matter of sidedness, elastic movement pulses in frantic parataxis, heartbeat presses sexual meter, a guest on the alert for climax in a gigantic chime. Breakage makes me examine the fate of flowers as something orgasmic, a sexual inclination to the human in everything (natural miasma, eruption, always as the head rediscovers projection, easy and evil and undone as a child in the ocean). In order to survive your curse, eat the fruit with your idiot face, or better yet love, let orgasm be less than a perception of ends. We move easily to do the work of the sea, to carry us from the pole and terminus of salt, its weight and necessity. Mouths know more than breaking open to interiors. No one can collect any more in seedtime. Heat forms rhythms, exceeds every passage and knows to memorize each star as it breaks away from the purity it follows.

Most of the series is mass. Whoever writes beautiful letters writes breakage as with a ceaseless camera; the movements are quick and occur below, side to side, lifting in a pulsing movement that is quick and, after, to the rhythm of quick heat and pushing: fucking is more lovely than any gesture—the alarming entry of the head of the penis is calming. Breakage takes on new use and flowers are sexual organs that include the human among all of them (it's always this natural, always desire recaptured by design, built up by the fallen entry and exit of fucking, of the pulsation of the sea;—it's love, it's ocean). Consider the course of singing—of voice let loose and stupid—everything before gain is love, everything during orgasm is love and is only fact in its moment. Facts disperse with the air she exhales. We all move in the same air; currents carry it across the sea and we feel it deep as pollen and salt, it fills us up; here the split comes clear. In seedtime nothing grows alone. Color, form, rhythm: everything that flashes past the eye is its own exception, and man and star and dog break before nothing—everything has taken on the purest of forms.

Mold reeks in the humidity. The house darkens, markings on the floor are beautiful writings of breakage met in a camera's eye; the eye flies to what is near, counting on what can be counted out—the white tiles lend themselves to a pulsing beginning, the heat slogs into each seam, the dew eats the wood and grows to mildew beneath, the heat is alarming, seeping into and filling up each hallway. Breakage has never meant heat—that which accomplishes bloom seeks itself, organizes itself in a hum that means "underwhelm" (an organization of the stable shelves, all tied to studs buried in the wall, we turn to them to place our things on them, we meet them as a place to place parts of ourselves, and we see them sometimes as a place where our lives are in play). One can see this spilling out of heat as a curse, lifting us out of time, it is heat as orgasm sucking us to a torpor of warmth. We'll begin to look at it as lucky, as another source of life overseeing us, as the meting out of stuff sending us deep, implicating us in shape-shifting; signs of more and less borne in the broken things we place on them (the shelves again). Go on to seedtime when the ghost says to go. The little worms have a clear rhythm: they behave in a summery passage through the dirt outside—by this I mean that the stars come to hand, that I can lift breakage and know its dirge-like sound hovering over my head, worms breaking my house apart.

The most beautiful in the series. The beautiful writing characteristic of breakage is the dressing up of the photograph's pause; the movements of the hand are stopped at last and they cease their side to side, their up and down, and remain a movement of touch that touches, in two senses, the sense of touch and that of feel—the heart still holds a possible throb, a thrust and erotic desire—it is a gesture of the vein that the hand is alert to the motions inside the heart. Breakage between the two is like a flower, all its organs inside itself—and this includes the human exactly (nature is what we are, always trying again to reproduce, done up in dick and cunt, this is our sign). —Now we'll see the course of each song as that which came before us, as love, as orgasm and as seeing the song of our *there*. We are equal displacements, equally of air and of sea, and we are derived from a deep pollen that suffuses the earth. I am not inclined to implicate myself in such gross statement; I am equally a concept of depth and breakage, I'm everything. Anything planted in seedtime grows to color, form, rhythm: keep out what keeps you from grasping—the first man was already broken and open and nothing will get us to the end of our true form.

It shines as it rises. Breakage is characteristic, calligraphy when the camera looks away; the lines all become one, off and on, they sit on top of themselves and gain pulse to rend their beginnings hither and thither—the heat zooms and slogs and its zooming is a sexual hub settling around a gesture, an arm that catches nothing that tries to settle. Breakage a name that dies all over again, in its blooming sexuality—an organ sent wide and sliding into mankind, under an overpass I see (all is natural until it sells itself, until it wills itself to its own end, this design that recalls itself, an impudent phallus, a sight that gels into itself). The curse is song that tells everything about how it spills all over itself, it says, this soiled song, that it is organism over all the stars spilling over the lip of the sky. We see the height of it all as we lift ourselves under the sea, a bloodless tribe full of salt tasting the delicious swing of our shifting and breakage is a moral concept, we fail to fall into the broken earth we've dug. It's a kind of seedtime with the earth. Far be it from me to form rhythms: an author overruns me in order to gain on me in one hundred still standing years that break nothing down so that I might hold still in the height I've reached—it's form I reach for, form I fail at.

Egregious film. As each June has its end in glass placed in planes across the room, so we content ourselves to see our places occupied with drama in religion, religion in drama. A simple song contains one idea, and its flaw is its method to get out of itself. A witty song is obstinate, flaunting all the undercurrents of its own satire.

Glass is sign. Windows and the far-flung sound of crystal in the hand put side by side; they contain the opening of tragedy into religion, religion into tragedy. A unique song has one idea and it opens possibility into every node. A song of place, unstopping, aftertaste of salt and urge.

A crack in the atmosphere as it inverts and scoops down. Oh shit, I believe the windows are built of glass again and sure enough, newest care is plastered up against them, and its warming pane is enough to allow me further belief that activity is Godsend, Godsent, this is drama. Heat, engine, the heart is that that I've missed, not some little thing, not some little door. Even in this song I'm not yet a man, yet I can see the storm as climax

English is film. The windows and canyons our children wrote over on the glass are a sort of juxtaposition and contain the insight that drama is religious, i.e., religion is drama. Soul holds song as idea, and they are happy together. One chance to get alone with spirit, nothing more than hands, the current of sex.

To search is to gamble. Bugs fleck the screen in the window and the pane lifts and gains my eyes a wandering—and the day is a big star's force that lifts water from the earth; this is religious narrative with no climax, climax with no action rising to meet it. The engine in the car outside lies, it is only an idea, a veiling of light within it; it lurches; it stops and restarts. Its little white lie is denounced by the storm rolling in. I take a seat inside my home

Choosing each centimeter. The window makes its own schemes and turns me aside—I am juxtaposed and content with the precise place of my idols, the religion that arises, the drama. The only song I hear says I should contain an idea of blood's possibility as it fills me and empties me. A windy song, everything flying with an undercurrent of sit the fuck down.

I was rash, I hid in a palace of our own, or in a possible world, or in the East. Paint spilled and drawn—because we see, or if you know where pistons hide, it is official: we are the only muscles that move our mouths. There is only ever one window, it is decoration; we break it by throwing through it a fantastic number of rocks—glass shatters out into the city; the number, we realize, is various, and as we watch we realize we need the number on this side of the window and it is never going to refenestrate itself

To each child comes an owning to place, of everything annealed and magicked to the world in its uses. Foolish world; for what is here is here to be seen, or else we throw it on the floor or at the walls outside until it is broken; it is hot with ownership and seen as gaudy target—missile-cum-target, a split arrow—the door selects its décor and is spirit, it taunts our breakdowns, selects care over fantasy—it lets a draft in, admits lift as realization, there is nothing left to hold.

The palace of the golden child is this my own, a possible world somewhat to the east of me. I am the world's fool: because of this, I go on, I know we search points that point out, that I am only the things that pass through my teeth. My movements are only décor, breakage mounts in a regular way, ordered to combine with the ordering of my sight—we are always only realizations of what is given.

Ballast still hanging around, all the ladybugs begin to stink—this is a possible world, it orients me. The world overcomes me and it was always to be seen this way. When night came down and everything stopped speaking in a way I could understand, then burrowing became gaudy, the day shunted and arty. In the bugs is never a care, I see this now, I say that breakage is orientation, a wobbly fantasy when nothing is ever more than half-marked.

This is nothing I can begin again

The placed things chide me in the day that surrounds me, a world full of plausible disorientation. The anointed fool — though each thing stands in its own place, it zooms off, knowing the certainty of its glide, its indices as a site of Godlike dents in the air. I am sending myself off alone and decorated in breakage, mostly ordinary as much as I fantasize myself beyond the loneliness at the bottom of this pissed-off knowledge

A place where rascals hide, where they do what everyone around them does, or else possible land that orients all us failures. The world greases us all up; we're here to blow away, a voice sends us off to our own places, what we write ends up gaudy in our teeth. Sleep sells us or wakes us beautiful; breakage comes at us ordinary, something south of fantasy — in the middle of a moment we see we're all someway necessary.

I lied. It's true. The messages
I took I hate and yet light dances
so breakage has only begun
to spirit me away and fuck-all,
I'm frenetic. And every song
is merely eerier since the floor
is still a part of my resonance.

The turnings. Girls dance against the light, sort themselves out in breakage and go off stage as possibility, as conjuration, frenetic. This is an eerie song; this is silence at its eeriest.

Yes, this is an abrupt turn. We make what we are given, we gain what light sends, breakage admits sight, we become thus cursed, frenetic. Uncanny song uncanny lease of life.

The turnings around. Pick the rug back up and shake it around, shake it before the light, make it a sort of breakage, let it be seen as something you can possess, stretch it out thus, frantically. This here is possible zone, slightly less audible since it can only be heard.

A torque—my child is dancing and meeting light, his method is the broken mouth that he places food into, broken food, frenetic. My mouth, he says, says good-bye to the food, he washes it down with water, or else water causes him to smile quietly.

Turning	around	remains
too	much	light
to	singe	us
breakage	sends	us
again	to	sea
a	whichever	way
frantic.	Mysterious	song
more	when	silent.

Lake shines and light clatters across its surface, devilish, contrast between the quiet and the free forces of energy —vector, true-seeing, as good as the break in a photographer's lens that has him see a ray of light at a lesser slant, miles in the distance.

A chin juts out, you see it as diabolical as it explodes from the light in the hallway; it is contest to your bedtime serenity and it lifts you up against the cold air around you as energy—it bears down on you and strikes you as too much, everything is broken in the slats of light your falling eyelids let in—Swan song falling for miles at the foot of your bed.

The lug of the seen is diabolical explosion of sight: contrast between serenity and liberation activated by energy's ferocity — a lamp, presumably — a broken bench I sit on — photographs easy and exact to let me out into life.

Milk dripping from my chin is diabolical explosion in the light: I can taste it when my tongue slips down there and what freedom, what ferocious energy — the lap-up lights me up, and I guess that heartbreak is so simple, no? Something a doctor could see if he fixed an x-ray in the middle of my chest.

Lakes shine with diabolic starlight: a contrast to the serenity and ferocious lancing out of energy — relight the lamps, they are probably old and broken and we can take our pictures in lesser light twenty million more times.

Shine this way, see,
and in offshore light
all we know explodes:
every contrast stumbles us
serene and the heat
wastes what is given
as energy sun blocked,
blotted out — breakage
howls show of rays
that strew themselves in
the middle a photograph

I lie again, the bloom is abstract, it's over all these stitches, these rows of trees. Die, you motherfuckers, I'm all in stitches anymore, neglected in the richest tongue that you glug into your throat, reticulate back out. Fuck all your blown fabrications—you'll never hear this song, it's a garden in the blood-red backyard of your house—we'll dance each bend of each branch around your house. This is music laid bare, fire zips through air and you'll know nothing but fluid core, a breach in the ground, an idea of soil in the bursting of flowers.

Fire eventually overstands you in the picture. One model never in the picture tends to turn regularly toward the reticulation of her hand pointing toward the sun. There are colors that shine and then there are colors that burn, the agency of each is its own song, and all a garden in the fear of loss, a risen first man. Music calms the beast, fleshes him into day, a hymn and a hearing of God's flowering out.

Flowers, yes, with over-painted abstraction. My mouth is seed fathering no hung paintings nor regularity nor replacement. Each core I find is brilliant, a flower, a coupling of songs, a garden of flowers as dear to me as my seeing them for all they are is birthing forth. Music forces itself from the core; forces, since a flower pushing through is a hymn to God.

Flowers get sent out at last, they look spray-painted. The petals under paint still hold their regularity of veins, the leaves their reticulation. For each brilliant color is itself a flowering, an accomplice to what can be seen, a garden full of flowering so long as we see us beside it. Music begins to fire from color, a gospel of the flowering of God.

A blue world meets the heat sent out over the kids. The children have a patron in this heat, and snow never reclaims them to its network. Thus held in the clear-blown wind, the heat derives its name in their song, even turns itself into a blizzard blowing in the doorway, a huge word to learn. A stark music in the clearing, a hymn to dead flowers.

Flowers against what is already painted in the abstract. The models dance in front of the paintings of themselves and tend to turn in regular motions that keep them in rhythm with the colors that catch them—it is a garden of normal flowers we inhabit, a sight of ability. Music is the strangest companion of color,

God breaks everything into song.

We've acquired lights, a subtle effect on the broken surface of the sea — light like diamond, or like a candle's awkward balance. This water carries soft wind. Each break seeks light, a sound like the spheres, the movement of moonlight and sunlight, everything to its own broken position. A gigantic star intercedes, I find it on a map guided and pointed to by a center that explodes. Here fate functions in advance of debt, and velocity is just so: a model of center's spin. A true use of magic, a visible sign of the brokenness inviting us: I can only manage one perfect part.

Lights on the water, there is nothing to effect water-to-diamond, or there is no candlelight to dance water to boiling, or nothing will find water pulled from its first-made form, though there is still breakage in the light (so equal to the stars, it's over everything —or moonlight, or sunlight, everything in harmony and everything bleak). One huge star seems to stand in the way, with a halo and points of sound flung from its center. There is a function that stands before every being and which gives us all our attractions and velocities—our testaments are origins, geometries. There is no frank use of magic that we see in the world, that is, on the level of inevitable breakage—general and more than what follows, it sails below our mastery.

Light in the water, the effect of what water does to water-on-water and light is diamond and candle light that dances only on water, and only the water has edge to invite light. Each break of water allows what stars allow and makes my entry easy. The water rocks, back and forth, and it is itself as easy as moonlight, as the sun, everything in contrary harmony. I have seen the sun and the moon in the water at once. Huge star sitting in the middle of a wide road, with halos and points alike flowering as centers. The quick function of life is perhaps that of dream: an equal velocity: my master is an always new geometry. Magic is easy, frank—nature (*natura naturans*—we're all a part) is a sort of breakage that tends to the specific: we lament only the magnificent lesson

Light in the water, I oversee the heat braiding the water in diamond effect; the heat dances and is headlight-like, the water is open to the open door and the searching wind blazes the film up in words. The floor is broken, I see in this light the evenness of stars, dear, the light of man, the light of place, everything in broken harmony. Even the shadows are starry and central, the heat lights up a point of halo in the center of my body. I am product of architecture, I am sold on the heat, an even being held in place. Even the heat of me is broken open in the natural magic of seeing—it is a sort of brokenness that swoons me in wormy patterns of air around me, the sea dies and gets met in my ear, in the song that my hands stretch out to hold close.

Lights on the water, the effect of a roiling lake refracting light, or the light of a dozen votives flickering their reflections in a soft wind. Because the window is broken the lights all roll in the same tint, softly, working in the night, the light of suns, all in harmony calling holy, holy, holy. A smally enormous tint of light assembles me in its midst, with a halo of lights all around my center. To be turned to the front is to be turned around, and everything is glass: this is my modest geometry. I only use the most normal of magic, I see everything as a sort of breakage I inevitably inherit, and I'll move everything around — mastery is all around me.

Lights on the water, the burning effect on the sea is the diamond-like otherness of every coming together of each crazy ray of light; it's an awful drop of water that spreads and burns every which way under wind. It's breakage that sets this light gluttonously home, sternly, deathlessly, all of a piece with the earth, tag you're it and everything is bleeding harmony. A thick stem in the middle of all this, a wen on its bark, a halo pointing to its struggle to rise into air; with this I grow down into soil, get held up in wind at its height, go forward over the wrecked yard, its wants of weeds, and stumble over a word: geometry is mastery—a loss of words spills over me, the yard is wide and empty and. An overwritten gain, a natural sense of magic in art, breakage's death is a normal thing and norms make their own magic. After all, we die to grow larger, our art is guess, a better lasting, a longer genesis,

ACKNOWLEDGMENTS

Much of the work in this book (or portions thereof) has appeared, sometimes in different forms, in the following journals: *Diagram, Drunken Boat, E•ratio, Eleven Eleven, Fact-Simile, Free Verse,* the *Massachusetts Review, Natural Bridge, Otoliths, Pank, Pinstripe Fedora, Puerto del Sol,* and *SoandSo.* I am grateful to the editors and staff of these journals for their faith in the project.

I would like to thank, in particular, the members of the editorial and production staff of the Center for Literary Publishing for their incredible patience with the text and for their yet more incredible patience with me: I couldn't be happier with the result of their efforts, or with the generosity of their attentions.

I'd also like to thank, in large, for their unflagging support (and unflinching criticism) of this project: my folks (Stan and Diane Henderson), my friends (Rebecca Lindenberg, Donald Revell, Craig Dworkin, Karen Brennan, Kathryn Cowles, Geoff Babbitt, Marnie Powers-Torrey, et multi al.), my kids (Charlotte, Pete, Audrey & Alex), and my dear doppelgänger (Derek Pollard). The genesis of the words in here springs from them; the result and fault rest only with me.

And a special thanks to Marilyn Brakhage for her kindness in permitting these Songs into the light Stan Brakhage cast fifty years before.

This book is set in Apollo MT and Palatino Linotype
by the Center for Literary Publishing
at Colorado State University.
Copyediting by Drew Webster.
Proofreading by Karen Montgomery Moore.
Book design and typesetting
by Abigail Kerstetter.
Cover design by Kristin George Bagdanov.
Printing by BookMobile.